this world

in this world
over hill...
viewing spring blossoms

Kobayashi Issa
(1763 – 1827)

this world

**HAIKU SOCIETY OF AMERICA
MEMBERS' ANTHOLOGY
2013**

**CAROLYN COIT DANCY
EDITOR**

**HAIKU SOCIETY OF AMERICA
NEW YORK**

This World

Copyright © 2013 by Haiku Society of America
All rights revert to the authors on publication.

ISBN 978-0-930172-11-4

Each poem in this anthology was selected by the editor from five published or unpublished haiku and senryu submitted by current members of the Haiku Society of America. Each participating member has one poem in this anthology.

Production coordination: Mike Montreuil —
Les Éditions des petits nuages, Ottawa, Ontario

Cover Illustration: Dennis Burns
Cover Design: Claudia Coutu Radmore
Book Layout: Lynda Wegner — www.freshimage.ca

Printed by Ferguson Graphics, Carleton Place, Ontario

Contents

Introduction	7
Poems	
Land	9
Water	85
Sky	105
Publication Credits	142
Index to Poets	145

Introduction

A keen observer of the natural world, Henry David Thoreau wrote, "The question is not what you look at, but what you see."

In this anthology, members of the Haiku Society of America express what they see through haiku and senryu. Collectively, these poems celebrate the natural world that provides for our physical needs and sustains us spiritually. Through the poet's eyes, readers will see anew salamanders and buffaloes, a rain forest and houseplants, a puddle and rivers, the Milky Way and fireflies, and so much more.

Inspired by the anthology's theme of "en plein air," these poems are grouped according to the natural realms of land, water, and sky. Represented here are 316 poets from 41 states, four Canadian provinces, and thirteen other nations.

Carolyn Coit Dancy
Editor

LAND

the distant mountain
reflected in his eyes…
dragonfly

Kobayashi Issa

winter's morning
    the dog
        pulls me into it

Bett Angel-Stawarz
Barmera, South Australia, Australia

in new snow
like fresh footprints
my revelations

Ellen L. Clarke
Bernardsville, New Jersey

first ski
the weight of snow
bends the cedar

    Bryan Hansel
    Grand Marais, Minnesota

an infinity
of snowflakes
i shovel mine

    Deb Koen
    Rochester, New York

January thaw
not sure
what to wear

    Mike Montreuil
    Ottawa, Ontario

valentine's day
the warmth of old love letters
　　in the fire

　　Ben Moeller-Gaa
　　St. Louis, Missouri

　　old flame—
　　the smell of woodsmoke
　　in her hair

　　　　Jennifer Sheridan
　　　　Glenview, Illinois

feeling for the pulse deep winter

Lorin Ford
Melbourne, Victoria, Australia

paper snowflakes
cling to window panes
no two alike

Brenda Lempp
Madison, Wisconsin

spring thaw
snow angels become one
with the earth

Poppy Herrin
Laurel, Mississippi

spring evening —
smelling the newness
of the universe

Edward J. Rielly
Westbrook, Maine

boys leap
into mud puddles
spring equinox

Peg McAulay Byrd
Madison, New Jersey

early spring
a bleeding heart tattoo
on her triceps

Tricia Knoll
Portland, Oregon

ocotillo red
only in springtime
she dresses wildly

    Joan Prefontaine
    Cottonwood, Arizona

Boston Marathon
118th running
Flags at Half Staff

    Raffael de Gruttola
    Natick, Massachusetts

Jobim's music
rushes through my veins
waters of spring

> *Neal Whitman*
> *Pacific Grove, California*

mother's day
she draws an olive branch
on a postcard

> *Carla Shepard Sims*
> *Harvest, Alabama*

mother's garden
the line-up
of sealed Mason jars

> *Elizabeth Black*
> *Arlington, Virginia*

do I gather peonies
or do they gather me—
the summer garden

> *Penny Harter*
> *Mays Landing, New Jersey*

overgrown garden
nothing
left to say

> *Susan Godwin*
> *Madison, Wisconsin*

half-truth
sod clings
to the garden spade

> *Michele L. Harvey*
> *Hamilton, New York*

roughing it —
a screen door slams
across the lake

> *Robert B. McNeill*
> *Winchester, Virginia*

on the last walk
we find no berries to share
forked road

Anita Curran Guenin
San Diego, California

first cup of coffee
watching the sun
drink the morning dew

Rich Burke
Limerick, Pennsylvania

summer solstice
another bubble bursts
in my café au lait

> *Joseph Kirschner*
> *Evanston, Illinois*

bubbles rising
at the slightest stir
the jokester

> *Padma Thampatty*
> *Wexford, Pennsylvania*

speed dating
ten new faces
I see only yours

> *Olga Skvortsova*
> *Beijing, China*

diplomat's child —
she draws her houses
with wings

Kristen B. Deming
Bethesda, Maryland

my favorite doll
still talks when I pull the string
summer garage sale

Sari Grandstaff
Saugerties. New York

Back and forth
we play catch
over the roof

Bruce England
Santa Clara, California

popsicles
two schoolboys
cooling it

Michael Fessler
Sagamihara, Japan

thirty-one flavors
so much ice cream
so little time

Marcyn Del Clements
Claremont, California

summer shade
the boy in the tire swing
not going anywhere

Randy Brooks
Decatur, Illinois

cool shade
a rest becomes
the afternoon

David Caruso
Haddonfield, New Jersey

autumn . . .
the street light changes
from green to yellow to red

> *John Quinnett*
> *Bryson City, North Carolina*

sky lanterns . . .
my inner dragon
making wishes

> *Thomas Chockley*
> *Plainfield, Illinois*

long sun
someone playing flute
in a dark house

Frances Jones
Bend, Oregon

the ink brush
sounds louder
this moonless night

Dennis Burns
Rochester, New York

election year
tots on trikes
rear-end each other

> Robert Seretny
> Milford, Maine

election speech...
his leonine hair
shifts in the wind

> Elizabeth Fanto
> Timonium, Maryland

dumpster diving
for a favorite book
To Kill a Mockingbird

> Carolyn Noah Graetz
> New Orleans, Louisiana

moving words —
bold graffiti
on boxcars

      Ann M. Penton
      Green Valley, Arizona

Fifties night
a 45 spins
with a twist

      Karen O'Leary
      West Fargo, North Dakota

Tijuana beat
on his headset
leaf-raking

      Richard St. Clair
      Cambridge, Massachusetts

farewell party
her bright smile
and camouflage

Eric Arthen
Worthington, Massachusetts

last bite
of the windfall apple
gravedigger

Roland Packer
Hamilton, Ontario

deeper
into autumn
this winding path

Cara Holman
Portland, Maine

coffee percolating away the rest of my life

    Roberta Beary
    Bethesda, Maryland

    changing pillowcases
    perchance
    a change of dreams

        Marilyn Gabel
        Agawam, Massachusetts

    midwinter
    forsythia explodes
    with sparrows

        Phyllis Lee
        Sebring, Ohio

dead of winter
and yet I dream
of wild plums

> *Elizabeth Howard*
> *Crossville, Tennessee*

chance meeting
with a childhood friend
snowdrops

> *Maxianne Berger*
> *Outremont, Quebec*

about to blossom
we meet again by chance
under the plum tree

> *Margaret D. McGee*
> *Port Townsend, Washington*

blossoms
on the cusp of opening
second date

> *Jacqueline Pearce*
> *Vancouver, British Columbia*

your return
at cherry blossom time
double spring

> *Jim Applegate*
> *Roswell, New Mexico*

with each gulp of soda
looking at cherry blossoms

> *Jessica Tremblay*
> *Burnaby, British Columbia*

cherry petals
an old man sweeps
his neighbour's path

> *Sidney Bending*
> *Victoria, British Columbia*

cherry blossoms
inching his walker
along the path

> *Patty Hardin*
> *Long Beach, Washington*

cherry blossoms
another year
without him

>Polly W. Swafford
>Prairie Village, Kansas

buds swelling the ache of losing you

>Sheila Sondik
>Bellingham, Washington

Fukushima —
cherry blossoms in full bloom
a deserted village

>Yasuhiko Shigemoto
>Hiroshima, Japan

giving these irises
to the people of Japan
a new dawn

> *Cliff T. Roberts*
> *Sansom Park, Texas*

rain beaten
daffodils hug
earth's warmth

> *John-Carl Davis*
> *West Bend, Wisconsin*

my neighbor's
magnolia
—all is forgiven

> *Sondra J. Byrnes*
> *South Bend, Indiana*

      the way I know
      you are coming
      blossom rain

          S.M. Abeles
          Washington DC

finally a burst
of good news
forsythia

    Barbara Snow
    Eugene, Oregon

    forsythia
    the key that unlocks spring

        Gloria Ayvazian
        Northampton, Massachusetts

a blues harp
en plein air
the cloying lilacs

Ignatius Fay
Sudbury, Ontario

face deep in lilacs
breathing in breathing out
the fragrance of spring

Helen A. Granger
Corunna, Michigan

dandelions
from a small, dirty hand —
mother's day

Carolyn M. Hinderliter
Phoenix, Arizona

dandelion puffball
in her shaky hand
she makes a wish

Roy Kindelberger
Botwell, Washington

dandelions
before the reasons why
all blow away

Michele Root-Bernstein
East Lansing, Michigan

for the love of purple
mowing around the
volunteer violets

> *Terri L. French*
> *Huntsville, Alabama*

Queen Anne's Lace
blooming everywhere
for us commoners

> *Jimi Bernath*
> *Englewood, Colorado*

Queen Anne's Lace —
all of summer
in one seed cap

> *Mary Frederick Ahearn*
> *Pottstown, Pennsylvania*

driving through Kansas
twenty miles of sunflowers
to the gallon

> *Elinor Pihl Huggett*
> *Lakeville, Indiana*

sunflowers
face down
evening

> *Robert Ertman*
> *Annapolis, Maryland*

hydrangea —
over tea mulling the idea
of utopia

> *Patricia J. Machmiller*
> *San Jose, California*

morning glories —
my thoughts trespass
their slatted fence

> *Marylouise Knight*
> *Omaha, Nebraska*

August morning —
    the scent of September
        in the roses

> *Antoinette Libro*
> *Sea Isle City, New Jersey*

last bus
his welcome flowers
start to wilt

> *Victor P. Gendrano*
> *Seal Beach, California*

bell-shaped blossoms
litter the lawn
season finale

> *Leta Leshe*
> *Shreveport, Louisiana*

heavy snow
my mind a seedling
in the deep hush

> *Irene K. Wilson*
> *Lexington, Massachusetts*

furry catkins
early sign
of springtime

> *Sandra J. Nantais*
> *Griffith, Indiana*

alder in purple
the collared dove's coo
in every catkin

> *Thomas Powell*
> *Gilford, County Armagh, Northern Ireland*

bloodroot
a primal storm
in the offing

> *Anne Burgevin*
> *Pennsylvania Furnace, Pennsylvania*

A lone daffodil
Bravely lifts its head to face
Winter's last onslaught

> *Mollie Danforth*
> *Alexandria, Virginia*

daffodils in snow
the start of
marriage counseling

> *Mike W. Blottenberger*
> *Hanover, Pennsylvania*

lengthening March days
tease drifts from warm roadsides
ferns, released, unfurl

> *Kathleen Serley*
> *Wausau, Wisconsin*

>> spring green
>> is everywhere
>> but the crayon box

>>> *Victoria Witherow*
>>> *Salt Lake City, Utah*

lying in grass
after her Marathon
drifting cumulus

> *Joan Zimmerman*
> *Santa Cruz, California*

summer —
fresh raspberry stains
on my shirt

> *Jill J. Lange*
> *Cleveland Heights, Ohio*

another year
we hadn't planned on
wild huckleberries

> *Ce Rosenow*
> *Eugene, Oregon*

morning run —
        down the lane
scent of honeysuckle

        Lisa Porter
        Millstadt, Illinois

I'm thinking
what she's thinking
wild mint

    Stephen A. Peters
    Bellingham, Washington

leaves turning
my heart tries out
a new rhythm

    James A. Paulson
    Narberth, Pennsylvania

ornamental maple
more chickadees
than leaves

> *Tanya McDonald*
> *Woodinville, Washington*

in my bushes
the neighbor's leaf pile
autumn wind

> *Mary Wuest*
> *Arlington, Virginia*

a light dusting
on filigreed trees — a taste
for maple syrup

> *Julie Warther*
> *Dover, Ohio*

pine needles pressed in snow
the weight of a full backpack

> *Jeremy Pendrey*
> *Walnut Creek, California*

bare branches
yet in my heart
a red bird sings

> *Rebecca Paradis*
> *Mendota, Minnesota*

my neighbor
wants to know its name
kwanzan cherry

> *Bruce H. Feingold*
> *Berkeley, California*

after the storm
half a plum tree
still blooming

> *Jerry Dressen*
> *Arcadia, Indiana*

backlit by sun
hundreds of maple seeds —
a toddler twirls

> Doris Lynch
> Bloomington, Indiana

April mist . . .
trees fill up
with birdsong

> Lauren Mayhew
> Sommerville, Massachusetts

a chainsaw cutting straight through spring tranquility

Mimi Ahern
San Jose, California

a brown gash
on the green hillside —
my judgment clear cut

Vicki McCullough
Vancouver, British Columbia

midsummer
the yearling spruce
dwarfed by fireweed

Connie Hutchison
Kirkland, Washington

dark of the moon —
    watching the grain rise slowly
        out of the stained wood

Marjorie Buettner
Chisago City, Minnesota

        fresh cedar chips
        I jump off the swing
        into childhood

Christina Nguyen
Hugo, Minnesota

pine forest
pasque flower trail
to the port-a-john

Patricia Nolan
Colorado Springs, Colorado

old cherry tree
lost a limb . . .
one more season

Janis Lukstein
Los Angeles, California

his old tree-house
still there
the scent of cedar

Chandra Bales
Albuquerque, New Mexico

in auvers-sur-oise
van gogh walked
and I am moved

Cheryl Anderson
Kenilworth, Illinois

bamboo grove . . .
the simmering sound
of afternoon rain

Jerome Cushman
Victor, New York

wet sidewalk
tickled by pink boots —
skipping child

> *Ellen Peckham*
> *New York, New York*

after the rain
the driveway blooms
with chalk art

> *Matthew D. Murphy*
> *Eagan, Minnesota*

spring breeze —
a red pinwheel spinning
on a child's grave

> *Kathe L. Palka*
> *Flemington, New Jersey*

in colorful shorts
we stare
at penguins

Mike Shaw
Midlothian, Virginia

summer daze
kickin' the can
down a red clay road

Charles Bernard Rodning
Semmes, Alabama

music
and hamburgers —
summer park

>*Maria Santomauro*
>*Commack, New York*

peanuts
on the picnic table
bluejay bluejay bluejay

>*Karen Stromberg*
>*La Mesa, California*

on the merry-go-round
with my daughter
a few fallen leaves

> *Michael Dylan Welch*
> *Sammamish, Washington*

lit up on
the blue beach
a deserted ferris wheel

> *Gene Myers*
> *Rockaway, New Jersey*

bandshell concert
a sea of sunglasses
waves with the music

> *Elizabeth Bodien*
> *Kempton, Pennsylvania*

Father's Day
in the park
balls everywhere

> *Caroline Giles Banks*
> *Minneapolis, Minnesota*

two years in box seats
behind home plate
where was the moon?

> *Johnye Strickland*
> *Maumelle, Arkansas*

a walk-off home run
up and over
the prison wall

> *Johnny Baranski*
> *Vancouver, Washington*

summer heat—
windmill palms
line the road

Joette Giorgis
Port St. Lucie, Florida

back in the Ozarks
unpacking my suitcase . . .
Yucatan heat

Gaylia Dalton
Fayetteville, Arkansas

on the lawn
enjoying the breeze
two empty chairs

    Denise Fontaine-Pincince
    Belchertown, Massachusetts

hefting a plum—
I know by heart
my father's orchard

    Michael McClintock
    Clovis, California

at the fence
we tell our stories . . .
the old horse and I

    Joan Vistain
    Antioch, Illinois

ethnic fair
around the world
in one night

> *Renee Londner*
> *Prospect, Connecticut*

raking gravel
at sundown
I comb the shadows

> *David Gershator*
> *St. Thomas, Virgin Islands*

oyster fungus
path to the homeless camp
wider and wider

> *Sheila K. Barksdale*
> *Gainesville, Florida*

ginko walk . . .
all the shades
of a haijin's words

> *Charlotte Digregorio*
> *Winnetka, Illinois*

Santa Fe
lingering scent of lilacs
after winter solstice

> *Mary Ann Newkirk*
> *Greer, South Carolina*

snow-dusted foothills —
scattering her ashes
where we hunted shrooms

> *Marilyn Sandall*
> *Seattle, Washington*

thin winter air
the hair left behind
in her brush

> *Michelle Schaefer*
> *Bothell, Washington*

Gettysburg
the hushed silence
of fallen snow

Gregory Longenecker
Pasadena, California

snowed in —
making milk
out of powder

Jim Kacian
Winchester, Virginia

Wisconsin spring
sandhill cranes
in a field of snow

Ellen Grace Olinger
Oostburg, Wisconsin

snowmelt
the green scent
of last year's alfalfa

Lesley Anne Swanson
Coopersburg, Pennsylvania

waves of prairie grass—
I hear the sea
in the wind

      Susan B. Auld
      Arlington Heights, Illinois

sweet breeze
from prairie flowers
birthday morning

      Del Todey Turner
      Waterloo, Iowa

ripping across the prairie
wildfire
in the lark's song

      Angela Terry
      Lake Forest Park, Washington

hope
is too big a word
garden morning

> Fonda Bell Miller
> Alexandria, Virginia

up the garden stairs the rising scent of rosemary

> Leslie Rose
> Shingle Springs, California

weeding the garden
oregano scent—
my grandmother's hands

> Kathleen O'Toole
> Takoma Park, Maryland

garden weeds—
she wipes the sweat from
under her breasts

> *Carmel Westerman*
> *Yuma, Arizona*

dragging a rake
the gardener wipes
his furrowed brow

> *Elizabeth Warren*
> *Owen Sound, Ontario*

rain-swept garden
the narcissus curls
into itself

> *Catherine Nowaski*
> *Rochester, New York*

a heartwood bench
draws me to it . . .
deepening spring

> *Judith Morrision Schallberger*
> *San Jose, California*

country teahouse
in between the flowerbeds
Canada Thistle

> *Jeanne Jorgensen*
> *Edmonton, Alberta*

freeway curves
a pause in the rhythm
of pines splitting sun

Richard Tice
Kent, Washington

flashing red light
our last vacation
together

Mary Ellen Rooney
New York, New York

mountain cabin—
the moon and a mouse
to welcome me

Carole MacRury
Point Roberts, Washington

campfire smoke
the rising song
of the thrush

CR Manley
Bellevue, Washington

South Rim
holding her baby out
to see

> *Richard M. Titus*
> *Alexandria, Virginia*

wilderness trail
that one moment
I felt lost

> *Stevie Strang*
> *Laguna Niguel, California*

switchbacks
up the mountain
we swap regrets

> *Brad Bennett*
> *Arlington, Massachusetts*

what remains
of the mountain
sand between my toes

> *Annette Makino*
> *Arcata, California*

our footprints
on separate beaches
the pull of tides

> *Deborah P. Kolodji*
> *Temple City, California*

dogwood blossoms . . .
learning to walk
without the dog

> *Julie Bloss Kelsey*
> *Germantown, Maryland*

spring yard work
my dog with a ball
in his mouth

> *John J. Han*
> *Manchester, Missouri*

small town —
the dogs
on Main Street

> *George Dortsy*
> *Yorktown, Virginia*

Sunday morning
a flowered hat
on the old mule

> Haiku Elvis
> Shreveport, Louisiana

empty
diamond . . . buffalo graze
at home

> Jim Aaron
> Arlington, Virginia

a monkey's leap

the forest canopy
shakes down its rain

> Ellen Compton
> Washington, DC

david and goliath
he attempts
to pill the cat

Mary Kipps
Sterling, Virginia

chattering squirrels
how still that tree
could be

Dorothy McLaughlin
Somerset, New Jersey

canyon crickets —
add to the list of sounds
he no longer hears

Alison Woolpert
Santa Cruz, California

shrilling crickets near dark
turn the earth

Kathleen Young Fenner
Menasha, Wisconsin

cicada skin —
that dream in which
she's still alive

Seren Fargo
Bellingham, Washington

little spider
clinging to my windshield
wild ride!!!

   Joanne M. Hogan
   Byfield, Massachusetts

    entangled
    in the life
    of the spider

      Thomas Martin
      Beaverton, Oregon

autumn equinox
salamanders cross the road
from both sides

   Marsh Muirhead
   Bemidji, Minnesota

looking for deer —
I miss a whole chapter
of the book CD

> *Adrienne Christian*
> *Greensboro, North Carolina*

white-capped peaks —
Holsteins huddle
by the fence

> *Ida M. Freilinger*
> *Bellevue, Washington*

the bay of hounds
echoes from deep woods
snow tracks

> *Lori Becherer*
> *Millstadt, Illinois*

Eating a rabbit
Drinking the Winter
I'll dream the rest of my drive

> *John T. Adams*
> *Southington, Ohio*

plains winter —
bison digging
through the snow

> *Mel Goldberg*
> *Ajijic, Jalisco, Mexico*

fresh snow
the cat prints
change direction

> Wanda D. Cook
> Hadley, Massachusetts

fresh snow
waiting for tracks
New Year's Day

> Alanna C. Burke
> Santa Fe, New Mexico

WATER

high noon--
the reed thrush sings
to a silent river

Kobayashi Issa

old pond
a deep turtle's
bubble

> *David G. Lanoue*
> *New Orleans, Louisiana*

submerged log an octave of turtles

> *Lori Lang*
> *Decatur, Georgia*

        mosquito larva
        on the stagnant pool —
        future Buddhas

            William Shehan
            Chicago, Illinois

Palm Sunday
the swimming pool fills
with the faithful

    Michael Henry Lee
    St. Augustine, Florida

        lost lake
        trees hide
        our secret

            Dorothy Coraggio
            Palm City, Florida

gliding past cattails
      ducks
glance at the hunter

> *Donna Buck*
> *Beaumont, California*

white caps
on Lake Champlain
a frank exchange of ideas

> *Deb Baker*
> *Concord, New Hampshire*

a trout jumps
from shallow water
with its shadow

> *IW. Crow*
> *Tokyo, Japan*

trout season
the warmth we add
to a cold river

> *Glenn G. Coats*
> *Prospect, Virginia*

favorite trout stream
she casts his ashes
to the evening rise

> *Jeff Stillman*
> *Hobe Sound, Florida*

petroglyphs the river cloudy through cottonwoods

> *Cherie Hunter Day*
> *Cupertino, California*

mangrove swamp . . .
the way a light shaft finds
minnows

> *Paula Moore*
> *Jacksonville, Florida*

the talk
my son throws stones
into the river

> *Tom Painting*
> *Atlanta, Georgia*

that river between us blackest night

Renée Owen
Sebastopol, California

mile-wide river
the evening sky fills
with the cries of swifts

Charles Trumbull
Santa Fe, New Mexico

frog song
in waterfall's thunder
evening duet

Diane de Anda
Playa del Ray, California

longest day of the year
barges move upriver
one   lock   at   a   time

Valorie Broadhurst Woerdehoff
Dubuque, Iowa

the crisscross
of ferryboats
oh what a night

William Scott Galasso
Edmonds, Washington

      wind trails on the sea
      tempt me   also
      to walk on water

Arch Haslett
Toronto, Ontario

   icy . . .
   slipping under
   the deadline

Pamela Larson
Arlington Heights, Illinois

winter wind
the sailboats pull harder
on their moorings

Joseph Robello
Novato, California

low tide
seashells beached
in the children's shoebox

> *Michael Moore*
> *DeSoto, Texas*

tidal pool
these same feelings
day in day out

> *Simon Hanson*
> *Allendale, South Australia, Australia*

break of dawn
starfish scattered
on the sand

> Bill Kenney
> Whitestone, New York

blow hole
the sea leaps
into the air

> Patricia Prime
> Te Atau South, Auckland, New Zealand

children's laughter
lifts with each wave —
early summer

> Dennis Holmes
> Saint Simons Island, Georgia

after a haircut
light-headed
with spring rain

> *Tom Tico*
> *San Francisco, California*

after the rain
smell
of childhood

> *Amelia Cotter*
> *Chicago, Illinois*

riding bikes
with our tongues out —
summer rain

> *Nicholas Magnus Sola*
> *New Orleans, Louisiana*

summer downpour . . .
we skip the pizza
for new trainers

> *John Kinory*
> *Steeple Ashton, Oxfordshire, United Kingdom*

all day rain—
the see-through petals
of rose of Sharon

Tzetzka Ilieva
Marietta, Georgia

summer rain . . .
the potted plants
push against the glass

Robert Witmer
Tokyo, Japan

ghost of
a white gazebo
night rain

> *Ann K. Schwader*
> *Westminster, Colorado*

autumn chill
the spaniel shakes rain
back into the night

> *Billie Wilson*
> *Juneau, Alaska*

pausing in mid-sentence . . .
a dry creek bed
waiting for rain

> *Bonnie Stepenoff*
> *Cape Girardeau, Missouri*

> only enough rain
> to count the drops—
> false hopes

>> *Scott Wiggerman*
>> *Austin, Texas*

silent morning
tule fog softens the edges
of my waking

Michael Sheffield
Kenwood, California

en plein air
the brushstrokes
of morning mist

Carolyn Coit Dancy
Pittsford, New York

sunlit ground fog
my ribcage rises and falls

> *Carmen Sterba*
> *University Place, Washington*

absorbed
by my journal page
morning fog

> *Lois J. Funk*
> *Manito, Illinois*

SKY

looking pretty
in the hole of the paper door…
Milky Way

Kobayashi Issa

Spring sun
I almost forgot
...the warmth

Jim Laurila
Florence, Massachusetts

september light in each face time

Dietmar Tauchner
Puchberg, Lower Austria, Austria

autumn sun —
my shadow merges
with those of the pines

Rob Dingman
Herkimer, New York

thistledown clouds
wrapped in swollen sun
solstice

Patricia Kennelly
Colorado Springs, Colorado

The longest night reveals
stars strewn overheard and within
a cloud of silent breath.

Carol Moyer Shearon
Ambler, Pennsylvania

winter solstice—
I walk the labyrinth
of my mind

> *Michael Morell*
> *Havertown, Pennsylvania*

winter sun
warmth of a smile
from a stranger

> *Jennifer Sutherland*
> *Melbourne, Victoria, Australia*

daybreak . . .
all the shades of brown
in the desert

> *Bruce Ross*
> *Hampden, Maine*

solstice —
light and dark curled
at the leaf's edge

Leanne McIntosh
Nanaimo, British Columbia

echoes barking
deep from hollow
call of jays to dawn

Nancy Scott Campbell
Palm Springs, California

meadowlark —
all you'll ever need to know
about sunrise

Chad Lee Robinson
Pierre, South Dakota

first sunrise
many passengers
topside

Dan Daly
Ballwin, Missouri

gull's cry . . .
the sequoia treetops
fog-filled

brett brady
Pahoa, Hawaii

husbanding
the last of the light
lone white crane

Brandon Bordelon
Baton Rouge, Louisiana

In late afternoon
pigeons pace the corrugated roof
the sun falls easily

> *Philip Boatright*
> *Tuscon, Arizona*

gold in them thar hills—
Sierra Madre
last light

> *Jay Friedenberg*
> *New York, New York*

aspen leaves flutter against a thick orange sunset

> *Jackie Hofer*
> *Longmont, Colorado*

twilight sky
his favorite place
without him

> Patricia M. Harvey
> East Longmeadow, Massachusetts

lingering afternoon
the ebb and flow
of birdsong

> Robyn Hood Black
> Gainesville, Georgia

morning haze
a flock of wild turkeys
disappears

Maria Borrelli
Orange, Connecticut

summer stillness
a hummingbird's wings
fan my dreams

Carolyn Hall
San Francisco, California

only a thin glass between us shimmering hummingbird

Peggy Heinrich
Santa Cruz, California

aria —
the hummingbird's throat
at sunset

> *Bill Pauly*
> *Dubuque, Iowa*

birds chattering
in a secret language
the Yiddish of childhood

> *Belle Shalom*
> *Bellingham, Washington*

relearning
nature's tongue —
spring birdsong

    Matthew Caretti
    Mercersburg, Pennsylvania

towhee's song —
we scan the meter
of a poem

    Lenard D. Moore
    Raleigh, North Carolina

here and there
chikadee dee dee dee
my thoughts exactly

    Mac Greene
    Indianapolis, Indiana

a chickadee sings
the black-and-white notes
winter keyboard

Art Elser
Denver, Colorado

birdsong no warble ever off key

Suzanne Niedzielska
Glastonbury, Connecticut

the cost
of birdseed repaid
birdsong

Dennise Aiello
Benton, Louisiana

barred owl
the echo
through open windows

Tamara Higgins
Jeffersonville, Vermont

below rice fields
hawks hitch the wind
kathmandu valley

William Hart
Montrose, California

hawk
on unseen wire
fog alert

Marian M. Poe
Plano, Texas

snow moon
the red-tail's eye grows
another year darker

Merrill Ann Gonzales
Dayville, Connecticut

I look away
from the hawk's fresh kill . . .
tulips in bud

Ferris Gilli
Marietta, Georgia

evening sun
a crow stalking
his shadow

> *Lynne Rees*
> *Offham, Kent, United Kingdom*

almost spring
only a half-V
of honking geese

> *Deanna Tiefenthal*
> *Rochester, New York*

en plein air
life passes
an insect on the wind

S.T. Childers
Dade City, Florida

morning walk—
monarch butterflies
feast on Echinacea

Nancy Wells
Damascus, Pennsylvania

the to-do list
I never write
drifting monarch

> *Rita Gray*
> *New York, New York*

the bumbling bee
seemingly drunk with passion
dandelion bloom

> *Philip Allen*
> *Hartland, Wisconsin*

stealing sips
from the garden hose
a yellow-jacket

> *Barbara Hay*
> *Ponca City, Oklahoma*

illuminating
the garden Buddha
a firefly's green glow

> *Sylvia Forges-Ryan*
> *North Haven, Connecticut*

the doe
twitches her ears
fireflies

> *Ruth Holzer*
> *Herndon, Virginia*

fireflies
the stars in the embers

Stella Pierides
Neusaess, Bavaria, Germany

twinkle
in her eyes
fireflies

Jeff Hoagland
Hopewell, New Jersey

cicada
a pitch too high
for concentration

> *Kevin Goldstein-Jackson*
> *Poole, Dorset, United Kingdom*

cicada dusk
will I ever find
my voice

> *Christopher Patchel*
> *Mettawa, Illinois*

nightfall
Grandpa searches too long
for the North Star

> *Edith Muesing-Ellwood*
> *Bushkill, Pennsylvania*

> Aurora Borealis
> he describes it
> without blinking

>> *Naia*
>> *Temecula, California*

ancient starlight the gnarled oak filled with other worlds

> *Pris Campbell*
> *Lake Worth, Florida*

shooting stars
I forget
my stiff neck

      Lidia Rozmus
      Vernon Hills, Illinois

watching stars
I long for the one
my planet circles

      LeRoy Gorman
      Napanee, Ontario

returning comet—
movement within
a vernal pool

paul m.
Bristol, Rhode Island

evening walk
step by step
toward moonrise

John Zheng
Itta Bena, Mississippi

midnight
face to face
with the moon

Jeannie Martin
Salisbury, Massachusetts

new moon
he touches her hand
shyly

    Christina Laurie
    Falmouth, Massachusetts

gnarled vines
rising into a rosé sky
the half moon

    Dianne Garcia
    Seattle, Washington

    half moon
    across the ocean
    the same half

        Nu Quang
        Seattle, Washington

full moon
a hole in the sky
inside out

> *Tomoko Hata*
> *Winnetka, Illinois*

Crossroads
the Lunar Eclipse
in his eyes

> *Juliet Seer Pazera*
> *New Orleans, Louisiana*

the moon won't ask what you've done with your life

> *Marian Olson*
> *Santa Fe, New Mexico*

crowning
between the lambing sheds
a waxing moon

    Sara Winteridge
    Fordingbridge, Hampshire, United Kingdom

held by
the swaying bamboo—
moonlight dances

    Carole Ann Lovin
    Clearwater, Florida

the pull of the moon
thinking again
of the girl in the blue dress

    Michael Ketchek
    Rochester, New York

washed blue
this film of ice
day moon

Peter McDonald
Fresno, California

pink moon
the scent of phlox I stole
from Nana's garden

Margaret Chula
Portland, Oregon

Blooming jasmine scent
wafts in the desert moonlight
the purest essence

Jennifer Jennings
Marana, Arizona

condensing
in the copper kettle
maple moon

Autumn Noelle Hall
Green Mountain Falls, Colorado

not in the mood
to look on the bright side
spring moon

Susan Antolin
Walnut Creek, California

running
through the grass
a breath of spring

Wesley Willis
Eldon, Missouri

no wind
yet twigs are moving —
brown wren

Shelley Baker-Gard
Portland, Oregon

clear summer night —
my ex-wife's voice
when my daughter speaks

Lee F. Strong
Rochester, New York

constant summer wind
people keep asking me
if I feel well

> *Janelle Barrera*
> *Key West, Florida*

blistering heat
a red barn and silo
in need of paint

> *Adelaide B. Shaw*
> *Millbrook, New York*

before the storm
a rainbow ring
wraps the moon

> *Tom Trowbridge*
> *Edgecomb, Maine*

rainbow
the ripest pomegranate
too high to reach

    Bob Lucky
    Addis Ababa, Ethiopia

    rainbow
        fading
            to blue

    Peter Meister
    New Hope, Alabama

heat lightning
the slow burn
of wild ginger ale

> *Aubrie Cox*
> *Taylorville, Illinois*

heat lightning the way your hand rests on mine

> *Margaret Dornaus*
> *Ozark, Arkansas*

stormy night
a flash of enlightenment
in Basho's eye

> *Ernest J. Berry*
> *Blenheim, Marlborough, New Zealand*

my life
just a blip on the radar
autumn typhoon

Beverly Acuff Momoi
Mountain View, California

autumn clouds —
what I think I know
keeps changing

Susan Constable
Nanoose Bay, British Columbia

cold-weather tear what i didn't understand

    Scott Glander
    Glenview, Illinois

    coastal gale —
    the muted timbre
    of his snoring

        Jone Rush MacCulloch
        Milwaukie, Oregon

Flurry snowflakes gently
etch frosty angels
on my cold window

    Suzanne V. Surles
    Jacksonville, North Carolina

march cold snap
on top of crusted snow
a dried leaf scurries

> *Donald Skrivseth*
> *Minneapolis, Minnesota*

a cold wind
seeps inside my coat
winter speaks

> *Diane Duffy*
> *Louisville, Kentucky*

high winds, dust,
and snow flurries
Albuquerque at last

> *John Armstrong*
> *Colorado Springs, Colorado*

wind across the prairie
not a single desire
left in me

Francine Banwarth
Dubuque, Iowa

mandolin wind —
you wear it well
everything I own

Ernesto P. Santiago
Nueva Vizcaya, Philippines

Publication Credits

Abeles, S. M.	European Quarterly Kukai #1 (Spring 2013)
Angel-Stawarz, Bett	*Third Australian Haiku Anthology* (2011)
Ayvazian, Gloria	*The Nor'Easter* 15:1 (2008)
Banwarth, Francine	*Acorn* 29 (Fall 2012)
Beary, Roberta	*Mariposa* 28 (Spring-Summer 2013)
Bending, Sidney	2011 Vancouver Cherry Blossom Festival
Berry, Ernest J.	2013 North Carolina Haiku Society Award
Buck, Donna	*contemporary haibun on-line* Vol. 9:1 (April 2013)
Buettner, Marjorie	2011 Robert Frost Haiku Award
Burns, Dennis	*Amidst,* café nietzsche press (2007)
Caruso, David	*Modern Haiku* 38:3 (Autumn 2007)
Colón, Carlos	*Prune Juice* 1:1 (2009)
Compton, Ellen	*tracing the fern,* Press Here (2007)
Constable, Susan	*Magnapoets* No. 9 (2012)
Cook, Wanda D.	2007 Anita Sadler Weiss Award
Coraggio, Dorothy	*Haiku Hippodrome* 39 (May-June 2012)
Cotter, Amelia	*The Heron's Nest* XII:3 (September 2010)
Dancy, Carolyn Coit	Shiki Kukai (November 2012)
Day, Cherie Hunter	*The Heron's Nest* XIV:4 (December 2012)
Deming, Kristen B.	*Modern Haiku* 40:3 (Autumn 2009)
Dornaus, Margaret	*tiny words* 12:1 (November 2012)
Dortsy, George	*The Heron's Nest* XIV:4 (December 2012)
Fanto, Elizabeth	*With Cherries On Top: 31 Flavors from NaHaiWriMo,* Press Here (2012)
Fargo, Seren	*Mu Haiku* Issue II
Ford, Lorin	2013 HaikuNow! Award
Gilli, Ferris	*Modern Haiku* 41:3 (Autumn 2012)
Gorman, LeRoy	*Eye to the Telescope* No. 1 (May 2011)
Grandstaff, Sari	2012 En Grand Prix Haiku Contest
Hart, William	*Monsoon,* Timberline Press (1991)
Harvey, Patricia	*The Temple Bell Stops* by Robert Epstein (2011)

Holman, Cara	*Windfall: Seabeck Anthology* (2012)
Huggett, Elinor Pihl	*moonset* (Autumn-Winter 2009)
Ilieva, Tzetzka	*The Mainichi* – Tokyo (July 28, 2012)
Issa, Kobayashi	*The Haiku of Kobayashi Issa*, online archive of Issa poems by translator David G. Lanoue at haikuguy.com/issa/
Jones, Frances	2013 Oregon Asian Celebration
Kacian, Jim	2009 Robert Frost Haiku Award
Kenney, Bill	*Haiku Calendar 2013*
Kinory, John	*Envoi* 147 (2007)
Laurila, Jim	*New England Letters* 34 (May 2013)
Libro, Antoinette	*Frogpond* 15:1 (1992)
Longenecker, Gregory	*World Haiku Review* (December 2012)
Lucky, Bob	*Acorn* 27 (Fall 2011)
Machmiller, Patricia J.	*The Heron's Nest* XIII:4 (December 2011)
Makino, Annette	*With Cherries On Top: 31 Flavors from NaHaiWriMo*, Press Here (2012)
Martin, Thomas	*Modern Haiku* 42:3 (Autumn 2011)
McClintock, Michael	*Frogpond* 26:3 (Autumn 2003)
Meister, Peter	*South by Southeast* 5:1 (Winter 1998)
Miller, Fonda Bell	*A New Resonance* 7, Red Moon Press (2011)
Moeller-Gaa, Ben	*Modern Haiku* 44:1 (Winter-Spring 2013)
Momoi, Beverly Acuff	*Modern Haiku* 44:1 (Winter-Spring 2013)
Moore, Lenard D.	*Frogpond* 35:3 (Autumn 2012)
Muirhead, Marsh	*The Heron's Nest* XII:4 (December 2010)
Naia	*Simply Haiku* 4:3 (2006)
Owen, Renée	*Half the Moon, Half of Me*, Two Autumns Press (2012)
Packer, Roland	*Kokako* 8 (April 2008)
Painting, Tom	*Modern Haiku* 43:3 (Autumn 2012)
Palka, Kathe L.	*Modern Haiku* 40:3 (Autumn 2009)
Patchel, Christopher	*Acorn* 24 (Spring 2010)
Paulson, James A.	*bottlerockets* 13:2 (2012)
Peters, Stephen A.	*Modern Haiku* 44:1 (Winter-Spring 2013)

Poe, Marian M.	*Ouachita Life* (November 2009)
Powell, Thomas	*Blithe Spirit* 23:2 (June 2013)
Prefontaine, Joan	*Lifting the Sky: Southwestern Haiku and Haiga*, Dos Gatos Press (2013)
Roberts, Cliff T.	*We Are All Japan* (2012)
Robinson, Chad Lee	*Frogpond* 35:2 (Spring-Summer 2012)
Rosenow, Ce	*The Color of Water*, Two Autumns Press (2013)
Sandall, Marilyn	*Frogpond* 34:1 (Winter 2011)
Schwader, Ann K.	*The Heron's Nest* XIII:4 (December 2011)
Shigemoto, Yasuhiko	*Kō* 26:10 (Spring – Summer 2012)
Snow, Barbara	Shiki Kukai (March 2012)
Sterba, Carmen	*Whirligig* (April 2011)
Stillman, Jeff	*Frogpond* 32:1 (Wintr 2009)
Stromberg, Karen	*an island of egrets*, Southern California Haiku Group Anthology (2010)
Strong, Lee F.	*Five Seasons*, Rochester Area Haiku Group (2009)
Tauchner, Dietmar	*Frogpond* 36:1 (Winter 2013)
Tico, Tom	*Frogpond* 26:1 (Winter 2003)
Vistain, Joan	*Acorn* 29 (Spring 2013)
Witmer, Robert	*The Heron's Nest* XII:3 (September 2010)
Woolpert, Alison	*Mariposa* 28 (Spring-Summer 2013)

Index of Poets

Aaron, Jim, 77
Abeles, S. M., 36
Adams, John T., 82
Ahearn, Mary Frederick, 39
Ahern, Mimi, 52
Aiello, Dennise, 117
Allen, Philip, 122
Anderson, Cheryl, 55
Angel-Stawarz, Bett, 11
Antolin, Susan, 133
Applegate, Jim, 32
Armstrong, John, 140
Arthen, Eric, 29
Auld, Susan B., 68
Ayvazian, Gloria, 36
Baker, Deb, 89
Baker-Gard, Shelley, 134
Bales, Chandra, 54
Banks, Caroline Giles, 60
Banwarth, Francine, 141
Baranski, Johnny, 60
Barksdale, Sheila K., 64
Barrera, Janelle, 135
Beary, Roberta, 30
Becherer, Lori, 81
Bending, Sidney, 33
Bennett, Brad, 74
Berger, Maxianne, 31
Bernath, Jimi, 39
Berry, Ernest J., 137
Black, Elizabeth, 18
Black, Robyn Hood, 113
Blottenberger, Mike W., 44
Boatwright, Philip, 112
Bodien, Elizabeth, 59
Bordelon, Brandon, 111
Borrelli, Maria, 114
Brady, Brett, 111
Brooks, Randy, 24
Buck, Donna, 89
Buettner, Marjorie, 53
Burgevin, Anne, 44

Burke, Alanna C., 83
Burke, Rich, 20
Burns, Dennis, 26
Byrd, Peg McAulay, 15
Byrnes, Sondra J., 35
Campbell, Nancy Scott, 110
Campbell, Pris, 126
Caretti, Matthew, 116
Caruso, David, 24
Childers, S.T., 121
Chockley, Thomas, 25
Christian, Adrienne, 81
Chula, Margaret, 132
Clarke, Ellen L., 11
Coats, Glenn G., 90
Colón, Carlos, 77
Compton, Ellen, 77
Constable, Susan, 138
Cook, Wanda D., 83
Coraggio, Dorothy, 88
Cotter, Amelia, 97
Cox, Aubrie, 137
Crow, IW., 90
Cushman, Jerome, 55
Dalton, Gaylia, 61
Daly, Dan, 111
Dancy, Carolyn Coit, 102
Danforth, Mollie, 44
Davis, John-Carl, 35
Day, Cherie Hunter, 91
de Anda, Diane, 92
de Gruttola, Raffael, 16
Del Clements, Marcyn, 23
Deming, Kristen B., 22
Digregorio, Charlotte, 64
Dingman, Rob, 107
Dornaus, Margaret, 137
Dortsy, George, 76
Dressen, Jerry, 50
Duffy, Diane, 140
Elser, Art, 117
England, Bruce, 22

Ertman, Robert, 40
Fanto, Elizabeth, 27
Fargo, Seren, 79
Fay, Ignatius, 37
Feingold, Bruce H., 50
Fenner, Kathleen Young, 79
Fessler, Michael, 23
Fontaine-Pincince, Denise, 62
Ford, Lorin, 14
Forges-Ryan, Sylvia, 123
Freilinger, Ida M., 81
French, Terri L., 39
Friedenberg, Jay, 112
Funk, Lois J., 103
Gabel, Marilyn, 30
Galasso, William Scott, 93
Garcia, Dianne, 129
Gendrano, Victor P., 42
Gershator, David, 63
Gilli, Ferris, 119
Giorgis, Joette, 61
Glander, Scott, 139
Godwin, Susan, 18
Goldberg, Mel, 82
Goldstein-Jackson, Kevin, 125
Gonzales, Merrill Ann, 119
Gorman, LeRoy, 127
Graetz, Carolyn Noah, 27
Granger, Helen A., 37
Grandstaff, Sari, 22
Gray, Rita, 122
Greene, Mac, 116
Guenin, Anita Curran, 20
Hall, Autumn Noelle, 133
Hall, Carolyn, 114
Han, John J., 76
Hansel, Bryan, 12
Hanson, Simon, 95
Hardin, Patty, 33
Hart, William, 118
Harter, Penny, 18
Harvey, Michele L., 19
Harvey, Patricia M., 113
Haslett, Arch, 94
Hata, Tomoko, 130

Hay, Barbara, 122
Heinrich, Peggy, 114
Herrin, Poppy, 14
Higgins, Tamara, 118
Hinderliter, Carolyn M., 38
Hoagland, Jeff, 124
Hofer, Jackie, 112
Hogan, Joanne M., 80
Holman, Cara, 29
Holmes, Dennis, 96
Holzer, Ruth, 123
Howard, Elizabeth, 31
Huggett, Elinor Pihl, 40
Hutchison, Connie, 52
Ilieva, Tzetzka, 99
Issa, 1, 9, 85, 105
Jennings, Jennifer, 133
Jones, Frances, 26
Jorgensen, Jeanne, 71
Kacian, Jim, 66
Kelsey, Julie Bloss, 76
Kennelly, Patricia, 108
Kenney, Bill, 96
Ketchek, Michael, 131
Kindelberger, Roy, 38
Kinory, John, 98
Kipps, Mary, 78
Kirschner, Joseph, 21
Knight, Marylouise, 41
Knoll, Tricia, 15
Koen, Deb, 12
Kolodji, Deborah P., 75
Lang, Lori, 87
Lange, Jill J., 46
Lanoue, David G., 87
Larson, Pamela, 94
Laurie, Christina, 129
Laurila, Jim, 107
Lee, Michael Henry, 88
Lee, Phyllis, 30
Lempp, Brenda, 14
Leshe, Leta, 42
Libro, Antoinette, 41
Londner, Renee, 63
Longenecker, Gregory, 66

Lovin, Carole Ann, 131
Lucky, Bob, 136
Lukstein, Janis, 54
Lynch, Doris, 51
MacCulloch, Jone Rush, 139
Machmiller, Patricia J., 41
MacRury, Carole, 73
Makino, Annette, 75
Manley, CR, 73
Martin, Jeannie, 128
Martin, Thomas, 80
Mayhew, Lauren, 51
McClintock, Michael, 62
McCullough, Vicki, 52
McDonald, Peter, 132
McDonald, Tanya, 48
McGee, Margaret D., 32
McIntosh, Leanne, 110
McLaughlin, Dorothy, 78
McNeill, Robert B., 19
Meister, Peter, 136
Miller, Fonda Bell, 69
Miller, Paul, 128
Moeller-Gaa, Ben, 13
Momoi, Beverly Acuff, 138
Montreuil, Mike, 12
Moore, Lenard D., 116
Moore, Michael, 95
Moore, Paula, 91
Morell, Michael, 109
Muesing-Ellwood, Edith, 126
Muirhead, Marsh, 80
Murphy, Matthew D., 56
Myers, Gene, 59
Naia, 126
Nantais, Sandra, 43
Newkirk, Mary Ann, 64
Nguyen, Christina, 53
Niedzielska, Suzanne, 117
Nolan, Patricia, 53
Nowaski, Catherine, 70
O'Leary, Karen, 28
Olinger, Ellen Grace, 67
Olson, Marian, 130
O'Toole, Kathleen, 69

Owen, Renée, 92
Packer, Roland, 29
Painting, Tom, 91
Palka, Kathe L., 56
Paradis, Rebecca, 49
Patchel, Christopher, 125
Paulson, James A., 47
Pauly, Bill, 115
Pazera, Juliet Seer, 130
Pearce, Jacqueline, 32
Peckham, Ellen, 56
Pendrey, Jeremy, 49
Penton, Ann M., 28
Peters, Stephen A., 47
Pierides, Stella, 124
Poe, Marian M., 119
Porter, Lisa, 47
Powell, Thomas, 43
Prefontaine, Joan, 16
Prime, Patricia, 96
Quang, Nu, 129
Quinnett, John, 25
Rees, Lynne, 120
Rielly, Edward J., 15
Robello, Joseph, 94
Roberts, Cliff T., 35
Robinson, Chad Lee, 110
Rodning, Charles Bernard, 57
Rooney, Mary Ellen, 72
Root-Bernstein, Michele, 38
Rose, Leslie, 69
Rosenow, Ce, 46
Ross, Bruce, 109
Rozmus, Lidia, 127
St. Clair, Richard, 28
Sandall, Marilyn, 65
Santiago, Ernesto P., 141
Santomauro, Maria, 58
Schaefer, Michelle, 65
Schallberger, Judith M., 71
Schwader, Ann K., 100
Seretny, Robert, 27
Serley, Kathleen, 45
Shalom, Belle, 115
Shaw, Adelaide B., 135

Shaw, Mike, 57
Shearon, Carol Moyer, 108
Sheffield, Michael, 102
Shehan, William, 88
Sheridan, Jennifer, 13
Shigemoto, Yasuhiko, 34
Sims, Carla Shepard, 17
Skrivseth, Donald, 140
Skvortsova, Olga, 21
Snow, Barbara, 36
Sola, Nicholas Magnus, 98
Sondik, Sheila, 34
Stepenoff, Bonnie, 101
Sterba, Carmen, 103
Stillman, Jeff, 90
Strang, Stevie, 74
Strickland, Johnye, 60
Stromberg, Karen, 58
Strong, Lee F., 134
Surles, Suzanne V., 139
Sutherland, Jennifer, 109
Swafford, Polly W., 34
Swanson, Lesley Anne, 67
Tauchner, Dietmar, 107
Terry, Angela, 68
Thampatty, Padma, 21

Tice, Richard, 72
Tico, Tom, 97
Tiefenthal, Deanna, 120
Titus, Richard M., 74
Tremblay, Jessica, 33
Trowbridge, Tom, 135
Trumbull, Charles, 92
Turner, Del Todey, 68
Vistain, Joan, 62
Warren, Elizabeth, 70
Warther, Julie, 49
Welch, Michael Dylan, 59
Wells, Nancy, 121
Westerman, Carmel, 70
Whitman, Neal, 17
Wiggerman, Scott, 101
Willis, Wesley, 134
Wilson, Billie, 100
Wilson, Irene K., 43
Winteridge, Sara, 131
Witherow, Victoria, 45
Witmer, Robert, 99
Woerdehoff, Valorie B., 93
Woolpert, Alison, 79
Wuest, Mary, 48
Zheng, John, 128
Zimmerman, Joan, 45